THE SEA AND THE HONEYCOMB

THE SEA
AND THE HONEYCOMB

A Book of Tiny Poems

edited by
ROBERT BLY

Beacon Press   Boston

Library of Congress catalog card number: 75-156447

International Standard Book Number: 0-8070-6410-6 (casebound)
0-8070-6411-4 (paperback)

Beacon Press books are published under the auspices
of the Unitarian Universalist Association

Published simultaneously in Canada by Saunders of Toronto, Ltd.

Printed in the United States of America

CONTENTS

v

III THE DEAD ON THEIR BACKS

IV ISSA

V IF YOU ARE STILL ALIVE . . .

DROPPING THE READER

The strength of a new form is that it makes both poet and reader aware of feelings they'd hardly noticed before. Most of the emotions we have are brief: they appear suddenly and vanish. They are a part of the swift life of the intelligence. Poetry in the English language has not developed any form that really responds to the rapidity and swiftness of our emotions. The epigram is not a poem but a versified idea. The shortest poem which has been respected in the English language is the sonnet; the result is that poets have tended to become insensitive to emotions that are too brief for such a poem, which means they are in fact insensitive to three quarters of the emotions they have.

Of course there are other emotions, that endure for hours or days, even for lifetimes. The poet in English tries to make his poems out of these. He has then either to disguise his brief emotion, or to link it with some extraneous material.

Many of the manuscripts we have of early Greek lyric poets like Alcaeus come down from copies made by scholars in Alexandrian libraries. Sometimes a scholar, after he had copied a brief, intense poem of Alcaeus, written several hundred years earlier, would add to it a composition of his own in the same meter, embodying his own thoughts upon reading the

ix

poem. Oddly enough today the same poet writes both parts. If he is skillful in rhythm and tone, the link is almost unnoticeable. An epigram is actually a piece written entirely by the Alexandrian scholar. It is a commentary on a suppressed poem.

An Alexandrian scholar is lurking inside most American poets: the American poet sitting at his desk writes a fine, intense poem of seven or eight lines, then a hand silently appears from somewhere inside his shirt and hastily adds fifteen more lines, telling us what the emotion means, relating it to philosophy, and adding a few moral comments. The invisible scholar is outraged at the idea of anyone writing a brief poem, because he is hardly able to get his chalky hand out of his cloak before the poem is over!

A brief poem does without the scaffolding of secondary ideas. Because of this, it moves more swiftly than the longer poem and with more intellectual exhilaration.

Paradise Lost is a good example of the long poem. Milton is always there, holding his hand beneath you. He doesn't want you to fall. When angels appear, he suggests the proper attitude to take toward angels. In short, he tells you what to think. He has a huge hand underneath you. In the brief poem, it is all different: the poet takes the reader to the edge of a cliff, as a mother eagle takes its nestling, and then drops him. Readers with a strong imagination enjoy it, and discover they can fly. The others fall down to the rocks where they are killed instantly.

The poet who succeeds in writing a short poem is like a man who has found his way through a stone wall into a valley miles long, where he lives. He walks back up the valley, and opens a door in the wall for an instant to show you where the entrance is. The more imaginative readers are able to slip through in the twenty or thirty seconds it takes to read his poem. Those who expect the poet to give them ideas see only a vague movement on the side of the mountain. Before they have turned all the way around to face the poem, the door is closed.

Readers of recent poetry are used to staggering along under lines swelled with the rhetoric of philosophy courses, experiences under mind-expanding drugs, new criticism—in short, the world of prose. They find it hard at first to concentrate on a short poem, but eventually they learn to find some value in being dropped.

Robert Bly

THE SEA AND THE HONEYCOMB

I

HORSEHAIR IN THE WILD ROSE BUSHES

SALVATORE QUASIMODO

AND SUDDENLY IT'S EVENING

Everyone is alone at the heart of the earth
pierced by a ray of sunlight:
and suddenly it's evening.

Translated by Charles Guenther

3

FALL

The shuffling mists, morning and evening.
The old oak stands there and coughs.
How easy it was to breathe during the days
The gold wagtails collected horsehair in the wild rose
   bushes.

Translated by Robert Bly

THE STORM

Each flower opened its mouth in the darkening air,
feeling about for the breasts of the abundant rain.

Meanwhile the armies of black-skinned clouds, loaded
    with water,
passed by majestically, bristling with the golden swords
    of lightning!

Translated by Robert Bly

Sometimes I go about pitying myself,
and all the time
I am being carried on great winds across the sky.

Chippewa language, adapted from the translation by
Frances Densmore

D. H. LAWRENCE

THE WHITE HORSE

The youth walks up to the white horse, to put its halter
    on
and the horse looks at him in silence.
They are so silent they are in another world.

ABU–L–HASAN ALI BEN HISN

THE GLOW OF WINE

The wine pierced by sunlight reddens
the fingers of the water carrying it,
as the antelope's nose is stained by juniper.

Translated by Robert Bly

THE MOLE

There is a mole on Ahmad's cheek that draws all
    those who are not now in love;
It is like a rose-garden, whose gardener is an
    Abyssinian.

Translated by Robert Bly

JUAN RAMÓN JIMÉNEZ

Music
A naked woman
running mad through the pure night!

Translated by Robert Bly

ANTONIO MACHADO

It is good knowing that glasses
are to drink from;
the bad thing is not to know
what thirst is for.

Translated by Robert Bly

Why should we call
these accidental furrows roads?
Everyone who moves on walks,
like Jesus, on the sea.

Translated by Robert Bly

II

DIVINITIES OF THE SNOW

THE OWL

My poor heart is an owl
That is nailed, unnailed, renailed.
I have run out of blood and energy.
I praise all those who love me.

Translated by Patrick Herriges

THE FLY

Our flies know all the tunes
They learned from the flies in Norway—
Those shaman flies that are
The divinities of the snow.

Translated by Robert Bly

ANTONIO MACHADO

If it is good to live,
then it is better to be asleep dreaming,
and best of all,
mother, is to awake.

Translated by Robert Bly

RENÉ CHAR

TO THE TREE–BROTHER WITH A FEW DAYS LEFT

Small harp of the larch trees,
On the buttress made of moss and growing flagstones,
—edge of the forests where the cloud breaks—
resonating note of space, in which I believe.

Translated by Robert Bly

This slowly drifting cloud is pitiful;
What dreamwalkers men become.
Awakened, I hear the one true thing—
Black rain on the roof of Fukakusa Temple.

Translated by Lucien Stryk and Takashi Ikemoto

GHALIB

In this world of infinite possibilities
I look around for the second step
of desire!
All I see is one foot-print!

Translated from the Urdu
by C. M. Naim and Robert Bly

WALNUT

Walnut: compressed wisdom,
tiny vegetable turtle,
brain of an elf
paralyzed for eternity.

Translated by Philip Silver

UNKNOWN ANCIENT GREEK POET

The moon has set
and the Pleiades;
midnight, hours pass, and I
lie down alone.

Translated by David Leviten

ANTONIO MACHADO

White inn,
the traveller's room,
with my shadow!

Translated by Robert Bly

Near the flowering mountain
The immense ocean is seething.
In the comb of my honey bees
There are tiny grains of salt.

Translated by Robert Bly

III

THE DEAD ON THEIR BACKS

LOOK DOWN, FAIR MOON

Look down, fair moon, and bathe this scene,
Pour softly down night's nimbus floods on faces ghastly,
    swollen, purple,
On the dead on their backs with arms tossed wide,
Pour down your unstinted nimbus, sacred moon.

GUILLAUME APOLLINAIRE

THE LION

O lion, mournful image
Of kings sadly brought down,
You are born now only in cages
In Hamburg, among the Germans.

Translated by Robert Bly

RENÉ CHAR

THE ORIOLE

3 September 1939

The oriole entered into the capitol of the sunrise.
The sword-point of his singing closed the saddened bed.
It was all over forever.

Translated by Robert Bly

AT THE DESK

I spent the entire day in official details;
And it almost pulled me down like the others:
I felt that tiny insane voluptuousness,
Getting this done, finally finishing that.

Translated by Robert Bly

THE RUNNER

On a flat road runs the well-train'd runner,
He is lean and sinewy with muscular legs,
He is thinly clothed, he leans forward as he runs,
With lightly closed fists and arms partially rais'd.

STÉPHANE MALLARMÉ

FANS

To Mme. Ponsot

Wing, take the place of her hand, shelter
from the sun or the sultry air
the face of Marguerite
Ponsot, who is watching the sea.

Translated by Charles Guenther

GALLEY WITH OARS

There seems to be nothing in the hold but snakes
that came in during the time of Noah, for fear of the
     deluge;

and now feeling the water rise to its level
each snake flicks its tongue out of an opening.

Translated by Robert Bly

ANTONIO MACHADO

People possess four things
that are no good at sea:
anchor, rudder, oars
and the fear of going down.

Translated by Robert Bly

ANTONIO MACHADO

In the sea called woman
few men shipwreck at night;
many at sunrise.

Translated by Robert Bly

Lord, you took from me what I loved most.
One more time, oh God, hear me cry out inside.
Lord, your will was accomplished against my own.
Lord, now my heart and the sea are standing alone.

Translated by Robert Bly

IV

ISSA

ISSA

Insects, why cry?
We all go
that way.

Translated by Robert Bly

This line of black ants—
maybe it goes all the way back
to that white cloud!

Translated by Robert Bly

Cricket, be
careful! I'm rolling
over!

Translated by Robert Bly

THE PIGEON MAKES HIS REQUEST

Since it's spring and raining,
could we have a little different expression,
oh owl?

Translated by Robert Bly

An ardent woman
and winter seclusion—
what a nation!

Translated by Robert Bly

Lanky frog, hold
your ground! Issa
is coming!

Translated by Robert Bly

ISSA

Why mention people?
Even the scarecrows
are crooked!

Translated by Robert Bly

The old dog bends his head listening . . .
I guess the singing
of the earthworms gets *to* him.

Translated by Robert Bly

I look into a dragonfly's eye
and see
the mountains over my shoulder.

Translated by Robert Bly

Now listen, you watermelons—
if any thieves come—
turn into frogs!

Translated by Robert Bly

V

IF YOU ARE STILL ALIVE . . .

THE TORCH

On my Northwest coast in the midst of the night a
  fisherman's group stands watching,
Out on the lake that expands before them, others are
  spearing salmon,
The canoe, a dim shadowy thing, moves across the black
  water,
Bearing a torch ablaze at the prow.

A FARM PICTURE

Through the ample open door of the peaceful country
   barn,
A sunlit pasture field with cattle and horses feeding,
And haze and vista, and the far horizon fading away.

SAINT GERAUD

SLEEP

We brush the moon that is not there.
Its caves come out and carry us inside.

SAINT GERAUD

DEATH

Going to sleep, I cross my hands on my chest.
They will place my hands like this,
it will look as though I'm flying into myself.

On nights like this the heart journeys to other islands.
Beaches rise and dance naked under moonlight.
Inland, asleep, you see
The stone face of your solitude being piled slowly.

When our hands are alone,
They open, like faces.
There is no shore
To their opening.

GOODBYE

If you are still alive when you read this,
Close your eyes. I am
Under their lids, growing black.

Only the birds are able to throw off their shadow.
The shadow always stays behind on earth.

Our imagination flies:
we are its shadow, on the earth.

Translated by Robert Bly

EARTH HARD

Earth hard to my heels
bear me up like a child
standing on its mother's belly.
I am a surprised guest to the air.

I STAND AND LOOK

I stand and look in the dark under a cloud,
But I see in the distance where the sun shines,
I see the thin haze on the tall white steeples of the city,
I see the glistening of the waters in the distance.

VI

THE HILL IN THE MIST

JOSÉ JUAN TABLATA

THE MONKEY

The little monkey looks at me . . .
He wants to tell me something—
that he has forgotten!

Translated by Robert Bly

SHIKI

The ferryboat, with a bull
on board, slides
through the winter rain.

Translated by Robert Bly

Millionaires,
come and drink of this clear water,
bears too.

Translated by Robert Bly

SHIKI

There are high clouds
over the dry slough
where the python lives.

Translated by Robert Bly

FRIGHTENING THINGS

The bark of an oak tree.
A place where there has been a fire.
The prickly water-lily, the water-chestnut, and the
　　chestnut burr.
A man with lots of thick hair who washes and dries it.

Translated by Ivan Morris

BASHÔ

The sea grows dark.
The voices of the wild ducks
turn white.

Translated by Robert Bly

BASHÔ

The temple bell stops—
but the sound keeps coming
out of the flowers.

Translated by Robert Bly

BASHÔ

Storm on Mount Asama!
Wind blowing
out of the stones!

Translated by Robert Bly

Dried salmon
and Kuya's breakthrough into the spirit—both
belong to the cold time of the year!

Translated by Robert Bly

BASHÔ

It's spring, all right;
that hill we never named
is hidden in the mist.

Translated by Robert Bly

VII

LOVE POEMS

WHITENESS

Never have I seen or heard of anything like this:
A pearl that changes out of modesty into a red jewel.

Her face is so white that when you look at its beauty,
You see your own face under its clear water.

Translated by Robert Bly

SEEDS

How many people I am good to, not because I like them,
or because I don't like them, but for a special reason!
The affection I give them is intended for another,
like the seeds we set out in a trap to catch birds.

Translated by Robert Bly

THE DAWN

When the dawn arrived with its light, and I saw it
shake off from its clear forehead the drops of the dew,

I said to my darling: "I am afraid the sun will discover
   our secret!"
She said to me, "I am afraid my brother will find me!"

Translated by Robert Bly

My mother
sent me to draw water
alone, and at such an hour.

Translated by W. S. Merwin

CALL IT ROMANCE

Call it romance, call it love,
you did it.
Now pull up the blanket,
I want to sleep.

Translated from the Pashtun
by Sadudin Shpoon

Little Mary
the wagon people call me;
they call me Little Mary . . .
I leave town with them.

Translated by Robert Bly

HER VISIT DURING SLEEP

The spirit came to the bed of the earnest lover,
despite all guards and chaperons.
I passed the night merry and ecstatic.
The joy of the night visit made me forget the joy of
    being awake.

Translated by Robert Bly

IBN HAZM

MEETINGS OF THOSE IN LOVE

The meeting that has to be secret reaches
an intensity that the open meeting cannot reach.
It is a delight that is mixed with danger
like walking on a road over moving sandhills!

Translated by Robert Bly

IBN HAZM

SEPARATION BY DEATH

She was pure and white, resembling the sun as it rises.
All other women were merely stars!
Love for her has made my heart fly off its permanent
  branch.
And after stopping a while, it is still hovering in the air!

Adapted by Robert Bly
from the translation by A. R. Nykl

AZEDDIN EL MOCADECCI

And sometimes we look to the end
of the tale, where there should be marriage-feasts,
and find only, as it were,
black marigolds and a silence.

Adapted by Robert Bly from the translation by
Edward Powys Mathers

ORIGINALS OF POEMS IN
FOREIGN LANGUAGES

ED È SUBITO SERA

Ognuno sta solo sul cuor della terra
trafitto da un raggio di sole:
ed è súbito sera.

Salvatore Quasimodo

HÖST

De släpande dimmorna, morgon och afton.
Där står den gamla eken och hostar.
Hur lätt det var att andas den gången
når gulärlan plockade tagel i törnrossnåret.

Werner Aspenström

LA TORMENTA

Cada flor abría en la oscuridad su boca, buscando
las ubres de la lluvia fecunda.

Y los ejércitos de las negras nubes, cargadas de agua,
desfilaban majestuosamente, armadas con los sables dorados
del relámpago.

Ibn Suhaid, the Grandson
Translated from the Arabic by García Gómez

EL REFLEJO DEL VINO

El reflejo del vino atravesado por la luz colorea de rojo los dedos del copero, como el enebro deja teñido el hocico del antílope.

Abu-L-Hasan Ali Ben Hisn
Translated from the Arabic by García Gómez

EL LUNAR

En la mejilla de Ahmad hay un lunar que hechiza a todo
    hombre libre de amor:
Parece un jardín de rosas cuyo jardinero es un abasinio.

Al-Muntafil
Translated from the Arabic by García Gómez

    ¡La música;
    —mujer desnuda,
    corriendo loca por la noche pura!—

    Juan Ramón Jiménez

Bueno es saber que los vasos
nos sirven para beber;
lo malo es que no sabemos
para qué sirve la sed.

Antonio Machado

¿Para qué llamar caminos
a los surcos del azar?...
Todo el que camina anda,
como Jesús, sobre el mar.

II

LE HIBOU

Mon pauvre cœur est un hibou
Qu'on cloue, qu'on décloue, qu'on recloue.
De sang, d'ardeur, il est à bout.
Tous ceux qui m'aiment, je les loue.

Guillaume Apollinaire

LA MOUCHE

Nos mouches savent des chansons
Que leur apprirent en Norvège
Les mouches ganiques qui sont
Les divinités de la neige.

Guillaume Apollinaire

Si vivir es bueno
es mejor soñar,
y mejor que todo,
madre, despertar.

Antonio Machado

VERS L'ARBRE–FRÈRE AUX JOURS COMPTES

Harpe brève des mélèzes,
Sur l'éperon de mousse et de dalles en germe
—façade des forêts où casse le nuage—,
Contrepoint du vide auquel je crois.

René Char

hai kahaaN tamannaa-kaa duusraa qadam, yaa rab
ham-nee daSt-e imkaaN-koo eek naqS-e paa paayaa

Ghalib
Phonetic transcription from Urdu by C. M. Naim

NUEZ

Nuez: sabiduría comprimida,
diminuta tortuga vegetal,
cerebro de duende
paralizado por la eternidad.

Jorge Carrera Andrade

¡Blanca hospedería,
celda de viajero,
con la sombra mía!

Antonio Machado

91

Junto a la sierra florida
Bulle el ancho mar.
El panal de mis abejas
Tiene granitos de sal.

Antonio Machado

III

LE LION

O Lion, malheureuse image
Des rois chus lamentablement,
Tu ne nais maintenant qu'en cage
A Hambourg, chez les Allemands.

Guillaume Apollinaire

LE LORIOT

3 septembre 1939

Le loriot entra dans la capitale de l'aube.
L'épée de son chant ferma le lit triste.
Tout à jamais prit fin.

René Char

AM AKTENTISCH

Da hab ich den ganzen Tag dekretiert;
Und es hätte mich fast wie so manchen verführt:
Ich spürte das kleine dumme Vergnügen,
Was abzumachen, was fertigzukriegen.

Theodor Storm

EVENTAILS

XVI

À Mme. Ponsot

Aile, mieux que sa main, abrite
Du soleil ou du hâle amer
Le visage de Marguerite
Ponsot, qui regarde la mer.

Juillet 93

Stéphane Mallarmé

LOS REMOS DE LAS GALERAS

Parece que no ocupan las bodegas más que serpientes,
desde que entraron, en tiempos de Noé, por miedo del diluvio,

y que, al ver que el agua sube de nivel,
cada serpiente agita su lengua por un agujero.

Ali Ben Hariq
Translated from the Arabic by García Gómez

Cuatro cosas tiene el hombre
que no sirven en la mar:
ancla, governalle y remos,
y miedo de naufragar.

Antonio Machado

En el mar de la mujer
pocos naufragan de noche;
muchos, al amanecer.

Antonio Machado

Señor, ya me arrancaste lo que yo más quería.
Oye otra vez, Dios mío, mi corazón clamar.
Tu voluntad se hizo, Señor, contra la mía.
Señor, ya estamos solos me corazón y el mar.

Antonio Machado

Mushi naku na   soko wa shonin no   hairiguchi

Ari no michi   kumo no mine yori   tsuzukiken

Negaeri wo   suru zo wakiyore   kirigirisu

Fukuró yo   tsurakuse naose   haru no ame

Kimi ga yo wa   onna mosu nari   fuyu gomori

Yase-gaeru   makeru na Issa   kore ni ari

Hito wa iza   sugu na kakashi mo   nakarikeri

Furu inu ya   mimizu no uta ni   kanji-gao

Tôyama ga   tsuki ni utsuru   tonbo kana

Hito kitara   kawazu to nare yo   hiyashi uri

Issa

V

Solo los pajaros pueden despegarse
de su sombra.
La sombra siempre es de tierra.

Nuestra imaginación vuela:
somos su sombra, en tierra.

Vladimir Nabukov
Translated from the Russian by Max Aub

EL MONO

El pequeño mono me mira...
¡Quisiera decirme
algo que se le olvida!

José Juan Tablata

Ushi tsunde   wataru kobune ya   yûshigure
Kanemochi mo   kuma mo kite nomu   shimizu kana
Uwabami no sumu   numa karete   kumo no mine

Shiki

Umi kurete   kamo no koe honoka ni   shiroshi
Kane kiete   hana no ka wa tsuku   yûbe kana
Fuki tobasu   ishi wa asama no   nowaki kana
Karazake mo   kûya no yase mo   kan no uchi
Haru nare ya   na mo naki yama no   asagasumi

Bashô

VII

LA TEZ BLANCA

Jamás vi ni oí cosa como ésta: una perla que por el pudor se transforma en cornalina.

Tan blanca es su cara, que, cuando contemplas sus perfecciones, ves tu propio rostro sumergido en su claridad.

Ibn Rabbihi
Translated from the Arabic by García Gómez

LOS GRANOS

¡A cuántas personas trato bien, no porque me agraden
ni me dejen de agradar, sino por una intención determinada!
El cariño que les muestro va dirigido a otro,
como los granos que se ponen en el cepo por cazar pájaros.

Ibn Hazm
Translated from the Arabic by García Gómez

EL ALBA

Cuando apareció la luz de la aurora y la vi sacudirse de su límpida frente el sudor del rocío, dije a mi amada: "Temo que el sol descubra nuestro secreto"; mas ello dijo: "¡A Dios no plazca que me descubra mi hermano!"

Sahl Ben Malik
Translated from the Arabic by García Gómez

Envíame mi madre
por agua, sola;
mirad a qué hora.

Anonymous, 14th century

Mariquita me llaman
los carreteros;
Mariquita me llaman...
voyme con ellos.

Lope de Vega

El espectro visitó al mancebo cuyo amor fué tenaz,
a despecho de vigilantes y guardianes.
Pasé mi noche alegre y regocijado.
El placer de la visión nocturna me hizo olvidar el de estar
despierto.

Ibn Hazm
Translated from the Arabic by García Gómez

La unión clandestina ocupa un lugar
a que no llega la unión posible y manifiesta.
Es un placer mezclado de precaución
como el andar por medio de las dunas.

Ibn Hazm
Translated from the Arabic by García Gómez

NOTES

Ibn Rabbihi was born in Cordoba in 860 and died there in 939 or 940. In 922 Ibn Suhaid, the Grandson, was born in Cordoba, and in 994 Ibn Hazm. Ibn Hazm is without question one of the greatest poets born in Europe. His work was enormous in range, including studies of politics, law, and theology. Three of his best known books were his *History of Religions,* his *Confessions,* and his *Ring on the Neck of the Dove,* or *The Book of Love.* This last book mingles poetry and prose and is a larger and earlier version of the *Vita Nuova.* The four poems of Ibn Hazm here are from this book. For one of the Ibn Hazm poems, I have used the translation, slightly adapted, by the American scholar A. R. Nykl. The rest of the poems I have translated from the Spanish versions made by the great Spanish scholar García Gómez.

García Gómez was born in Madrid in 1905, and was a student of Miguel Asin. Later with Asin he edited the review *Al-Andalus.* His translations of the small, elegant and intense poems of the Spanish Arabs were collected in a book called *Poemas Arabigoandaluces,* first published in 1930. This book had great influence on Lorca and other poets. Behind much Spanish poetry of this century, but especially the Andalusian, one can see the delicacy and richness of the Arab image. Gómez' *Poemas Arabigoandaluces* and his *Cinco Poetas Musulmanes* have been reprinted in the Colección Austral, published by Espasa-Calpe in Madrid.

Al-Muntafil was an eleventh century poet from Granada,

and Ali Ben Hariq a poet of two centuries later, from Valencia, who died in 1225.

Issa was a Japanese poet, born in 1763, who died in 1827. He is the greatest frog poet in the world, the greatest fly poet in the world, and maybe the greatest child poet in the world. More poems of his can be found in *A Year of My Life,* translated by Nobuyuki Yuasa, University of California Press, and in *Haiku* (four volumes) by R. H. Blyth, Hokuseido Press.

Saint Geraud is the pseudonym of a young Chicago poet, Bill Knott. Follett has published a volume of his poems, entitled *Naomi Poems: Corpse and Beans.*

The poem "I Stand and Look" is a poem of Whitman's that has just been turned up. It was printed in the Spring 1965 issue of the *Quarterly Review of Literature.* The other poems are from *Leaves of Grass.*

Robert Bly

ACKNOWLEDGMENTS